Portrayals of Hope and Beauty

A Collection of Poems

by

Brian Blackwell

Brian Blackwell

ISBN: 978-0-9565018-4-4

First published in 2014 by
Carillon Magazine
19 Godric Drive
Brinsworth
Rotherham
South Yorkshire
S60 5AN
www.carillonmag.co.uk

Printed in the UK by
Printdomain.net
107 High Street,
Thurnscoe,
Rotherham
S63 0QZ
www.printdomain.net

Cover image ©
website: Karl Blackwell
           Photography Correspondent
           http://karlblackwell.com blog
           http://karlblackwell.wordpress.com

I dedicate this anthology to Nick Occhioni, my daughter Anna's partner. They are the parents of my grandson Lewis. Nick is kind, energetic and a very supportive member of our whole family. His caring and helpful approach to those around him are unique, always positive and full of humour.

Brian

About the Author

Brian has been writing poetry as a serious activity for nearly 30 years now.

Around 50 editors have published his poems and he has produced 17 collections of his own work. His career as a teacher spanned almost 40 years, covering teaching posts in schools, colleges and universities. Initially he taught biology then re-qualified in psychology. Much of this latter discipline took place in three universities in Belarus where he was a part-time lecturer during the 1990s.

He is fascinated by the art of the last half century, classical music of the 20th century, and keeps up his scientific reading. In his 50s he ran 76 road races, 19 of them full marathons. Poetry and grand-children are dominating his retirement.

His humanism and psychology are clearly represented in his writing. Much of his work is political and philosophical, and reviewers have frequently remarked on his high command of the English language: rather odd for a mere scientist!

Portrayals of Hope and Beauty

If a picture has a countenance
dwell upon it. It represents perceptions
of the artist however transitory.

Poets keep to words, record life's quirks
and distractions, elevate dissension
to an art: a social amanuensis.

Musicians play on sounds; they hurtle
across ravines of silence, opening-up
susceptibilities to inspiration.

Every sight and sound are there
for observation, interpretation, exposing
creativity to minds of consequence.

Frosty twigs that scratch upon your windows
may aspire to presentations on a canvas,
on a violin, in a poet's journal.

Irrational or sorrowful, robust or dreaming,
inconsequential masquerades may be the essence
of love or grieving, portrayals of hope and beauty.

The Sense of Things

The colloquies of pseudo-intellectuals make you gasp:
their shrill and hectoring voices do not pacify.
They may at times just scratch the surfaces
of your personal desolation.

But what of parasitic unreality where scalpels cut
too near the nerve, where clouds of gloom meander
and maunder, interfere with rapport and
the solace of whispers?

The daguerreotype of images of grey upon grey,
will fuel the hunger for the real, deny despondency,
wrestle with malevolent intrusions.
I need to know the sense of things.

I wish to comprehend the hierarchy of metaphor
where there's never a leavening of spirits.
Traumas are conquered readily and one does not
have to defend one's point of view. To slither
on any scree, feel totally free.

This is the freedom that can override complacency,
generate one's personal integrity, temper
the whifflers, allow you to grow.

A Strange Compensation

You can be trapped by remorse, with its impetuous
repetitions of emotional wrath. The impotence
of pending grief and that fearful loss of love
are beyond all pain and indifference.

The withering frosts sustain your mental agitations,
your suffering is impregnable. No assistance or
sympathy can console. Your sleepless nights
are monotonous and stultifying.

But do not resort to those conceits of belief:
mendacious trickery to force you to blame
yourself, feel guilty, demean yourself
by deferential self-sacrifice to some fallacious
myth. Even an infestation of missionaries
has no lasting effect. Just laugh it all away!

Yet even then, laughter can be wearing:
a strange compensation after all the suffering.

This Contract

You've evolved this contract, this bonding,
an authorization to cuddle and caress,
to snuggle and smooch, to kiss and canoodle .

Entranced you'll agree to more; allow it to
happen. You'll no longer hesitate.

You'll embrace and nestle in each other's arms,
be curious of odours and fragrances from those
ejaculants of errors. You'll flirt and fondle
yet more. Let hormones interact and stimulate,
let them evoke their inevitable kicks and thrills.

Tickling tongues may wiggle and wriggle,
lips entangling passions, (don't mind the saliva),
so hold in closely, compress what your hands,
your wandering hands, can accommodate.

Those most calm and patient, tender-hearted,
will find those vital sensitivities. They'll
cultivate a ferment and enhance your sharing
possibilities, potential, your empathizing charms.

To Be Ourselves

Those scurrilous caricatures the press call
celebrities! Real people, real lives: but
do the rest of us need such presentations
and pantomime? Do these dramatisations
of lives aid the egos of those depicted?
Actors, singers, politicians... we'd
never wish to emulate them.

But what of envy? Do we need to seem
so deficient with our own styles of being?
Or do spurious interests keep us sane!
We may be short of cash and opportunities
but satisfaction, altruism, loving can't be
bought or borrowed. No need to emulate.
Best to be ourselves.

Your Masquerade

Intellectual pretensions may be your niggardly camouflage:
a sublimation of your feared anxieties. Is that a kind of
saraband to mock your bewildered opponents?

But why pretend? What have you to hide? Have you
anything to offer? Why create an image of superiority?
Even if superior, in measurable ways, your conduct will be
for someone else's claim and judgement.

If those others seem so small, inferior, pitiable, contemptible
why attack? To demoralise, knock confidence, humiliate,
is surely bereft of judgement and wisdom? Your masquerade
may be smart, but will it portray your veracity? Self-image?

Focus on Those You Love

The impalpable ash of your final passive act
will end all that you have ever known,
ever wished for, ever learned, ever forgotten,
ever expected. Think of these truths.

You can change what happens for the rest
of your life. Your implacable sweetness
and loving must have focus on those you
love. Don't leave anything for guesswork
or the negative outcomes of blind stubbornness.
Develop what is there, not what is not. Waste
no time on that which will never be there,
like the pathos and self-indulgence
of say songs of praise or prayer.

Cerebral Enclosures

They're like parasitic worms. They torture
your mind, create the vibrations
that echo round the labyrinths
of your skull. They generate pain.

Pain like that of a lost limb: it somehow
directs your consciousness, engulfs the silences,
pulses through your rib cage, deafens
the scouring impulses that charge your brain.

The neurones have the DNA of our consciousness,
the dissidence that makes us alive. Thence,
break from our dreary cerebral enclosures.

Life's Plankton

Life is a bed of ice. The more you reinforce it
the more it possesses you. Property fixations,
material commitments, doomed where love is concerned.

If all you aspire to is malice, however gentle, it is malice
just the same. This harms all benevolence
and wilful co-operation.

As soon as empowerment within a partnership becomes
inflexible, relentless, unforgiving you have to calculate
your odds. Shackles tighten and loosen; a mutual dilution
emanates; the selfishness of solipsism pervades.

Intellectual war can be, it is, so wearing. Crepitant nerves
will jostle and crack; tolerance fades. Shock waves
will swallow you: all anguish and dross will defeat you.
It's time to leave. Or you'll choke on life's plankton.

Hurtling Evolution

Dreams may embrace you, torment and savage
your tranquility, preclude your peace of mind.
Your sleep is no longer restful. It will not pacify.

The abrasions you suffer from sand in your shoes,
from shells that scrape and scratch your skin awaken
in you the wilderness fears of snakes and scorpions.

Your scope for relaxing is punctured: like the tearing
of flesh by vultures or wolves. Preparing perhaps
for another dream, cutting your mind to component
shards, slicing your trains of thought into molecules
of broken intellect, a dementia that blots out the clouds.

Yet plankton feeds huge whales! These Cetaceous beauties
are both harmonies and anomalies from hurtling evolution:
upheavals and creations, sifting the gems and reinventing
their strata of magnificence, like opals emerging from their
engulfing rocks. Fossils sleeping in their whispering rock-tiers.

Despair and Seething Misery

("love and affection are the great stupefiers and soporific." – Gerald Brenan)

Love and affection! How real are they?
Conceptual perhaps? Or just deceptive torments?
They start with a bang, but the bang they may end with
is often far louder.

Despair and seething misery often erupt.
Leaping into a friendship and fading out of it
can be hard to cope with, control. So achingly punitive.
It hurts; traumatises.

Agitation may arise, spiteful silences, and withering
manipulation. Is that your lot? Insoluble and appalling
exchanges can poison your air;
can choke your fluency.

So what of fidelity? Some say essential.
And what of infidelity? Some say acceptable!
But it usually tears the lovers apart.
Love and affection may be here to stay, but so are
murder and madness, superstition too.

A Seal of Concordat

Life is but a mirror of our perceptions,
with tedious nonsense and fewer erections.
But where would we be without the two of us
who savour the love, even when so often
seems unrequited?

We dodge from fantasies of lovers or some crazy
incubus. We depend so much on assenting closeness
whether pure or blighted. We're mutually crazy
out of sheer respect, despite all the accentuations
and too much fuss.

We suffer the ups and downs of unfortunate
neglect. Yet underneath all this we always know
we're waiting for that vital unrepentant
kiss, a seal of concordat, an approval of taste.

Life-blood Gets Tranquilized

("It is unsatisfactory to exist as a sort of mistletoe
on the life-blood of others." – Frances Partridge)

Mistletoe has long been involved in ritual, whether
pagan or purely secular. Quite apart from the kissing
games, as ancient as we know. It is a half-hearted parasite
on trees. Damages but rarely kills. In quantity may sap
their host-trees' resources. Blossom and fruit yields may
suffer, their life-blood gets tranquilized.

Like any rigidity and deprivation children too are disturbed,
benumbed, especially when fed with false verities: become
so crippled in their openness, disabled in adaptability and pliancy.

They soon become the puppets of control-freaks, dogged preachers
of defunct philosophies. Their minds become as fragile as
old lace, blanched as an almond. Nothing left to shine, nothing
left to trespass on the realms of creativity, ambition, fulfilment.

Far Better than Indifference

I've forgotten what I said and what
I'd written. Letters that followed made
reference to my offensive style. Far better
than indifference I guess.

Affirmation used to be so flattering.
I've passed that now. Yet people allow
their anger to foam. Like projectile
vomiting there's a kind of violence
that's expressed in such ordinary
behaviour, such ordinary behaviour.

By disagreeing they simply remind you
that you must surely disagree with them too.
But do they wish to take that on board?
Or are they rocked, disturbed, determined
to be heard?

Their views really count. But so do yours
and mine. However much they've been forgotten.
However much they say they hurt.

Free to Differ

If you're found lurking on the edge, the fringe
of your nebulous fantasies, take heed. Listen
for those silent soliloquies that urge you to declare
your love and compassion.

These are for friends who really matter.
They are the honest ones, loyal ones, prepared
 to take risks with their dedications, deliberations
and support. Try to understand those blemishes
of earlier years with all their distortions and caricature.

Let the felicity of self expression be extant, devoid
of humbug and prudery. There're times when justification
for agreeing with the views and philosophies of another
are tentative so long as you respect the author's
consistency and effort for clarity. Each and every
soupcon of detail needs comprehending. Yet you
and they are surely free to differ.

A Question of Space and Time

Is anything left now? Has trust finally gone?
To be bereft of trust creates a kind of vacuum.
Wherever has it all gone?

Can one feel the nature of this vacuum?
Or is it but a state of denial? Can it be
recognised, or be just enhanced awareness
of whatever is NOT there, or maybe wasn't?

Do gaps in one's recall get filled, or are they
buried deeper down? That would be defence
perhaps, or guilt; an alibi even, an attempt
to form a picture with a shortfall of components,
somewhat bankrupt. Like a spalled mosaic.
Disfunctions are so destructive. All accolades
then are defunct.

This Peculiar Continuity

Diligence is what they ask for;
diligence they sometimes get.
But what is the cost, this unattainable
goal for the few? For many some say.
This arbitrary target, this imposed pressure.

This invisible icon may be there or maybe
not. Perhaps it is. Perhaps it is on a receding
horizon. How do you define it? Recognise it?
Approach it? Know when you've arrived?
And what do you do when you meet it- head on?

Is diligence a way of working, a quality
in what you do? Is perseverance involved?
A sustained thoroughness? A compulsive drive?
Can it be slow or gentle? Are there rewards?
Has this industriousness a demand or outcome?

Diligence can drive you insane; you have to stop
in your tracks. Minds get blown, saturated, can
take no more. Maybe a fear of failure. Or a perceived
success they could not countenance. Isolated, success
or failure, you still have society to enter.

Will it accept you after the event? What happens if not?
Camouflage, stealth, retreat? Were we ever prepared
for this peculiar continuity, this grind, this escape?

Not at the Moment You Choose

Never feel inferior, there's nothing wrong
with fallibility. Brighter folk are simply
smarter with deceit! Be guarded.

Every darkness is low on light, cloud-thick,
waiting for the sunshine to pounce.
Most problems and fears may be expunged,
but not at the moment you choose.

No point in grieving for an undefined loss.
Even book-ends can be deprived of support,
the books of life between them gone. But
you can always reignite a snuffed-out lamp.

Just as icicles can kill, they can also melt,
reveal their valuable states, confront you,
make you think. Sometimes, too, allow
your fallibility to shrink.

In Kisses and Words

Tongue-tied, love-tied, encompassed by our lips:
the passions are moist and warm. Fermenting
fantasies may over-ride discretion,
may not want to fathom future entanglements.

Live your life right now, where inter-lacing,
inter-facing, interactions bubble
and brew. Love what's best, who's best now
for you. Embracing, kissing, gently hugging:
let ponderings, wanderings, meanderings,
bondings, become the heat of the earth.
Our mouths shall command all
in kisses and words.

Entangled Tongues

Entangled tongues may be seeking love: the sounds
of love; the words of love. They ferment in the sub-
conscious and enrich our dreams and fantasies,
steer our realities.

Those French-kiss-cuddles, like any writhing passions
still energise the harmonies of love: passivity in friendship
does not work. Real effort is required and has to be shared.
So don't delay your playful inventiveness.

And then, my love, don't misconstrue the language of silence;
no need to nurture those many doubts. Think of the concept
of love, the generative concept, so very much bigger than
physicality. Let tongues and kisses entwine;
let love prevail, inspire.

The Turmoil and Purring of Love

Life can be like a passionate duet, with its
ululating warbles, its guddle and mush,
and the dissidence that may at times inspire.

But the players are sometimes in separate
rooms; not just with different keys, but playing
conflicting tunes, atonal perhaps, or
something else indecipherable.

Their occasional harmonies may sometimes
not be compatible, the partnership losing out
from ill-conceived variations, over-editing,
indifference by critics.

These are the boulders displaced, but only
by earthquakes or landslides. The air displaced
can be deathly cold, unpredictable. Even
unresolvable. Something a lasting
love must overcome.

You'll Need More than Music

Tranquility: so tender, fragile,
ready to fall at a blink
like a skeletal leaf. The silence
is frangible. It needs to be protected
like an unborn child, already
absorbing the stimuli of survival
and selfhood.

You know not what a foetus can hear,
but music it must surely take in.
Perhaps it listens too and shares
with its mother. There'll be a kind of
connectedness. They'll sooth each other,
generate harmony. But you'll need more
than music, with time.

Kisses Endure

My mouth, my lips: these are the features
that guide my kisses. Welcome them!
They are warm, moist, trustworthy.

My tongue is the one that encompasses
your tongue. It makes my kisses comfortable
and lasting; sincere and passionate as the words
that give them permission to act and seek loving.

Kisses elsewhere can also have power and zest.
We can make our kisses genuine, meandering,
eternal, evocative. They'll trespass on doubts
and any insecurity, fill our world with enterprise
and curiosity, tell us that our world is under
our control.

Welcome my mouth and lips, for kisses endure.

Something We Must Not Lose

Love is stunning: can create such incredible bonding,
mutual harmony, respect. Other factors are involved too.
There's sharing, co-operating. It's not about control
but laissez faire, more scope, enabling a "give and take"
approach to life and living.

Yet doubts may well creep in! Fallacies like intuition,
superstition, small talk, quibbling, evasiveness. But watch
for that turbulent flip: the love of power may burrow in
like a fungus, replace the power of love.

There'll be divisiveness, inflexibility, an attempt at unilateral
control, intolerance, irrational competitiveness, the weakening
of mutuality. Thence the elements of domination.

Would reappraisal help? It may do. It can do. But often will
exacerbate divisions, pettiness, suspicion, even shards of paranoia.

A new appraisal may take time: a definition that allows
for qualitative variations, without too much judgementalism.
Or where is fulfilment? Something we must not lose.

Tranquility

Why not search for an enviable tranquility, devoid
of the humbug of self-deception and the mumbo-
jumbo of creed?

Look to a wilderness, deserts, distant mountains.
Maybe dry or hot, flooded or torn apart by tempests.
Desert rains dry fast like a piss in the sand.
Much like spilt blood, with its sickening fragrance,
yet free of the odours, synthetic odours of cities and towns.

These are the towns so cruel with their blandness, starkness,
indifference. Their aggressive harmonies imposed
by ill-thought-out regulations.

Quite unlike a Baobab flower: its quick smile dazzling
before the rains, an astonishing texture of velvet,
uniquely graceful and tender to the touch. A transience
so powerful, acute, stark as honeysuckle, importunate
as a cactus or crocodile. But a sign of desert.

Such deserts are so silent; a silence that flays all anguish;
it's the ultimate in sublime tranquility.

Desert Ants

No fear of heat in the hill's cramped space,
no fear of bright hot sand.
But what of the system within each mound
immune from all reason and grace?

Its fullness is quite unlike the heaviness
of slow unleavened bread yet is bursting out
from a picture frame's segmental view:
the unenclosed, the nothingness.

A ferment of expectation, a pus,
a caldron like a compost of leaves.
Each grain of sand a mountain
that each can move with little fuss.

Defines itself without emancipation;
reveals a kind of consciousness. Astonishing
to see such quirkish contradictions:
the routine peace, dynamic flux, a blip

of sophistication.

Curtains

I am closing my curtains
on autumn's gloom. Yet
the leaves are so colourful.

The insects are slowing down
now and birds from the fields
have had their fill. They're exploring
our gardens. But the gloom persists;
Winter is coming.

Winter has its rewards, my home
becomes cosy; like a bear's cave,
a squirrel's hide, or the snug cocoon
of an unborn moth or butterfly.

These warming wombs enable birth
in the Spring that follows. The birth
of new vigour, new aspirations.

The colours of delicate unfurling
leaves, emerging fauna, the brightness
of warming sunshine, a beauty their own.

I'll draw back my curtains
and welcome you in.

Fossils Sustain

Lives have been frisked for millennia,
amber eternity reflecting the scale of time.
These icons of heritage have determined
our here and now, anticipate whatever's to come.

Each fossil, a sarcophagus, a time-capsule
fixed, permanent, stable. Each will enrich
those perceptions of preservation, progression.
No longer have they vulnerability: their lives
have gone, terminated. Yet those fossils sustain.

Nature's Abundance

The susurrant hiss in an autumn wood
is calling for the black milk of winter.
Low temperatures and dampness prevail,
decay sets in. The foliage has fulfilled its role,
the outcomes are resources for Spring.
Their cabals of sedulous chemistry
have closed for winter.

There's no breach of faith for springtime. The buds
and blossoms erupt. The Summer glory and pendulous
crops will be there to behold. No esoteric caution:
just nature's abundance, luxuriance and splendour.

Each Silent Slug or Snail

Their radula is a mobile tongue, a resilient rasp
that files away at vegetation, injures your
magnificent flora, your luxuriant borders.

The silvery slime of slobbering slugs, and snails
with their hard-hats, has made its mark. They fell your
plants like timbermen, gnaw out the centres of favourite
flowers, like your prize chrysanthemums and peonies,
just to rest or breed.

Their slime reflects the moonlight, their mating
manufactures yet more, and poisons pump them dry.
Occasional thrushes eat a live one but take in some
poison too. Each silent slug and snail will sink
to its demise. Maybe a thrush or two too.

Tremulous Delight

Dusty with deference and boredom the winter woodland
is stark and spare. Woodland wildlife struggle in their poverty.
Their tiny vaults, ravines and cubbyholes are cold and bleak
and full of sparsity and rancour. Most somehow survive.

Springtime coughs itself erratically to warmth and brightness.
Fears and uncertainty of survivors vanish. They seek mates,
gallivant, peruse, declare, revivify; rear their offspring.
Such is nature's fragile certainty and tremulous delight.

This Inversion of Nature's History

Sunshine bids our garden postures: sitting
under fruit trees, a table for books and wine.
The myriad insects bomb us with excrement,
a stickiness pervades.

We are above such torment: sitting in a garden
is an inspiration all its own. Flowers galore, an ocean
of green leaves with their special shapes and textures.

The insect world alone is fascination. Many seek
nectar, others search for smaller creatures, prey for
carnivores. Caterpillars, oh so few now. Next year's
nocturnal beauty in the form of moths, and others;
the shrinking few of beetles and butterflies.

Even honey-bees are on the wane; fruit trees may suffer.
The hum and buzz if this wildlife is quieter now, shadowed
and slowed by mankind's misdemeanours and utter madness.

Older folk have memories; younger folk the Internet.
Different ways of challenging this inversion of nature's
history must be heralded anew. We know out time is short,
so why allow it to shorten yet more?

Let the Landscapes Be Left to Be

Landscaping is like giving a facelift
to a faded beauty, her skin reptilian,
her scraggy neck and cleavage like dried
seaweed. Why manicure a forest
or a wooded glen? Beauty has a presence
without the aid of man.

To change some natural everglade is
to crucify it. A regimented tree-scape is but
a crop, its serried ranks like wartime cemeteries.
But graves without their bodies, heads without
their helmets, ink on farewell letters
faded now, unreadable.

Middle-class folk may find it easier, taking their
dogs for their twice-daily craps, hiding them
under public seats, or plopping them into some bin.
Even neurotic hygienists would not think of disease,
let their pets sprawl all over them, lick them indeed.
Hardly wholesome even if largely benign.

The landscapes must surely be left to be.

No Second Chance

Those ghostly emanations of the misty mountains
evoke passion, passion with an edge. Yet still a hint
of anxiety. Forget the aromas of sorrow; forget the scars
of desolation and stony unreality. Ponder their natural
beauty, that ethereal continuum, the frets of emotion...
music to a muse, a paean for philosophers.

Mountains are upheavals from the wildest centres
of the earth, beneath the quakes, tectonic machinations,
the drift of nations. Their protean, atavistic, perpetual
change and evolution retain reality, develop a temporal
future. This is the world on which we rely, depend on.
We must accept it, enjoy it, protect it.
There's no second chance.

Something Endures

Exquisite openings of flowers in Spring,
tremulous as gold leaf, create your gardens of desire.
This beauty will not move mountains nor tame
the tides, but it will challenge conceits and lies
of pretentious preachers. It will however enhance
the silent magnificence of nature's opulence.

This may be but a sequence of flashes, but moments
worth eternities. Every palette of petals submits
to appreciation. An opal sky does not allow
too harsh a shadow, but magnifies serenity, powers
the tapestry of each and every stitch, a simple stitch.
But something endures, a presence, that you acknowledge.

Parameters of Creativity

Parasites on every tree, just itching to penetrate, to chew,
discolour, tear apart or slowly choke. Attacking leaves and buds,
bark and blossoms... A few were commensals – just there
for the ride or occasional help.

Algae, lichens, mosses, fungi, epiphytes and all, just clinging
to their hosts as timeless substrates, a place to live, survive
and die. On the way they grow, damage where they stay, multiply.
Their offspring live another day, and on to another tree.

Clambering ivy, clematis, bryony and honeysuckle simply climb,
unsure how far to go they rarely kill their handy tree.

A silent, patient oak receives its share of enemies, and those
just hanging on as somewhere to be. The occasional sweet
chestnut, beech or willow take their primal ration. The poplar
has its colonies of mistletoe, sheds its leaves in winter exposing
its kissing-machine to those who care to clamber up and steal it!

Then there are blossoms, fruits and beautiful foliage competing
for awareness by artists, writers, gardeners. Each to his or her
parameters of creativity, for their particular brand of joy.

All of a Feather

The Jays have no music in them. Just squawks.
But they do have colour and display it well.

Jackdaws are deemed pristine, yet destroy
the lives of other birds – their eggs and fledglings.

The Kite is magnificent: huge, elegant, yet
austere. It kills with precision. A flesh-eater
with power and swiftness.

The Goldfinch has perfection: so colourful,
eats just seeds, the occasional fly. But is loved
for its merry song, hour after hour,
except in the snow.

My friend the Black Woodpecker has style.
And beauty with its Rembrandt-red-rich crown.
It works with such sturdiness when it bores
its holes in Oak. Its raucous call has a harshness
about it, yet somehow seems playful too.
It yells out aloud as it approaches its nest
each evening. And reveilles each morning
as it starts each day.

Your Foibles and Quirks

As whatever we lose of our hearing disperses
a silence creeps in, unobtrusively, nibbling
at faint whisperings of insect mumblings,
or chatterings of fading birdsong.

And darkness, it creeps from below, from under
the trees, under stones and walls. As light shrinks
away the shadows elbow their way through branches
and wipe out the brushstrokes of clarity:
everything melts and merges.

The silences and shadows may enhance your edginess,
insomnia, paranoia. You cannot blame them: you
are the variable, the agent, the Higgs-Boson that holds
you where you are.

Signature Tune

(Cardiac ward, Burgundy)

Hospital window; silent vistas, 'til the birds awake.
Without the local language the loneliness
perpetuates, magnifies. The sun and moon
follow their usual arcs. Trees reflect their hues:
copper beech, silver birch, an oak and several
firs. So rich with their seasonal nuts and cones.

Indecorous rooks swirl about and land on fragile
twigs. Their offspring, scruffy already, crash-land
and tumble through the branches like damaged
kites. Leaping into the air is not the problem: it's
getting back that takes the time. They learn quite fast
the tuneless squawks of their parents, repeated
from early dawn 'til sundown – as if they're afraid
of forgetting their signature tune.

Captain Cook's Terra Nullius

I once saw a cow simply draped in a tree,
a victim of flooding, hanging like a haemorrhoid,
dead as a dolmen. Such is the power of flooding
creeks in the land of Australian Aborigines.

Yet those deserts inspire: so free of the sounds,
synthetic sounds, of toxic cities. The starlit skies,
the scuffle of lizards, the slithers of snakes, the distant
screeches and howls of wedge-tailed eagles, ready to
take on a feral camel or a newborn calf.

This is the land of the Aborigines where sacred sites
are interwoven with nature's grandeur.
Captain Cook was wrong. Australia is theirs.

Dust and Energy

We each appraise our personal state,
our gains and losses. No other creature
assesses its demise like woman or man.

This magma of chemical turbulence
is but a spit for the universe, indeed
a part of a spit. But to each and every one
of us that spit is life itself, our survival
from birth to death.

A finite flash of amazing complexity,
a violent turmoil of gigantic exchanges
that define our history, and all creativity.
Yet but a smidgeon of dust and energy.

Just Waiting to Happen

("Nothing in this world is too wonderful to be true" – Michael Faraday.)

Perhaps we should temper our impatience and our indifferences:
the reality of "Gaea", pure "Gossamer pavilions of earth's
biodiversity".*

Here are the incommensurable perspectives: we all fit
into this giant, global scheme. Interacting, competing,
differentiating, melding... a balance of succeeding
and failing.

Four billion years and still we squabble! A lot has gone wrong.
Repair work is slow, and much of that has failed. We must be
the only arbiters of these impediments. The myriad interfaces
fool many; only a few are dealt with adequately.

Many are not even recognised. Some think we've done it all,
others that we never will. Some of course have hypothetical,
superstitious remedies that are doomed from the start to fail.
Failure is their bent because they are gullible, deluded people.
Too rigid to seek evidence.

Even when heuristics seek and find, reliability is still at stake.
Truth can be so evasive. Yet the wonders of each and every
pavilion, each presentation, inspire the generations, activate
our curiosity.

So why seek accolades when love of life is there around you,
established, seeking no retribution, just waiting to happen?

* Those "interlocking of all ecosystems – the entire biosphere"
James E. Lovelock.

The Elegance of Reason

Reverence and deference have worried me awhile now.
They needed resisting: they nurtured conceit, concealed
a false awareness, created the emptiness of delusion.

They constructed umbrageous palisades that denied
or defied the enrichment and enlivening of amative
encounters, those pearls of fondness
and cosy warmth. Still do.

This is not about self-pity, a gangrene of attitude,
but an acknowledgement that those who insist
on reverence for their concoctions of philosophy
are deluded; somehow dishonest.

Dishonest with themselves, overconfident with false
appraisals. Their disturbed and distorted ideas of superstition
and supernatural mythologies confound them.

Their theological tangles of history blind them to the elegance
of reason. As for deference they suffer the arrogance of self-
importance to an unacceptable degree. Their personal
certainties are mere anomalies.

False certainties, anomalous to reason, are incompatible
with those mirrored events of droll history. A history of myths
and fantasies, a history of repetition, repetition, a refinement
of lies. Schemes of lies.

A refinement of quasi-logic. Are they not devoid of consistent
and tangible evidence? This reverence and deference still worry
me: need resisting. We're desperately short on love.

A Bower of Bliss

Who dares to live in a bower of bliss?
Isn't that where you find some gulf of indifference,
the maudlin and insipid gestures and postures
of apathy, the silliness of false protocol, dizzy
refinements? You'll surely find such louche
benignity and paralytic intransigence right there.

There is a time for liking or rejecting.
A time for wanting or avoiding. Then time
for needing yet fearing. Sheer bliss may be false!
Like eternity: a fantasy that lacks authentic scope.
Wake up and get real!

Anything but Stillness

How still is stillness? It activates recall
and those perceptual miscellanies you approach,
peruse, depart from... anything but stillness.

The lightning oscillations are flickering, reflections
passing like ghosts. Stillness is like nature's
agitations through a lens. All around becomes
enlarged and manoeuvred, however carefree,
however demure.

All around is movement and dance. Cameras
may fix a frame but the viewers
will call the tune.

Vastitudes of Vertigo

Unresolved intrigues may hold a particular pathos.
The darknesses of winter may trap you, fill a void
with emptiness, frighten you with vastitudes
of vertigo, even dubious desire.

Loneliness transpires for some, a seasonal evocation.
A suffocating emptiness. One maybe confined
to silences: no birdsong after all, just traffic, wind
and a clatter of tedious rainfall.

A pending snowstorm is but a single aspect
of winter. The frosty opalescence may have
aesthetic presence, simple ornaments of desire
for an occasional artist or poet.

There maybe too a blissful indifference to all
such threats, however unfathomable. Times occur
when the immediate dynamics are merely benign.
A spare intensity of neutrality is barely there,
virtually unnoticed.

Modulated Metaphor

Incipient certainties close doors, build barricades,
close minds. Such certainties are temporal, transient,
'til evidence transpires.

We know too well the hunger of delusional paranoiacs
for certainties that sound secure: accusations apocryphal,
judgements disturbed.

Yet pedantry is not enough; modulated metaphor
is dreamtime. Bizarre and banal replies to questioning
are too reassuring and too often false, disclaimed.

A Floating Collage

Our oscillating thoughts will generate new images,
new values. Spurious interpretations too, no doubt.
They'll juggle with juxtapositions, escape beyond
the usual frames of reference, cast new shadows,
illuminate crucial concepts, like effervescent
fantasies, raging desires.

The scale and tone of attributes and qualities, ideas
and principles, will form a floating collage. Much
like a reflection in a pond, that your mind can absorb,
interpret, disseminate. It will help to settle your mind;
enhance your frames of reference.

To Patch up the Flaws

Unbridgeable vacuums, hurt esteem,
you're so demoralized. What was it
that made you feel deflated, undermined?

Had you thought your intellect was
stretched too far, alertness and resilience
lacking? Perhaps you thought you were
not big enough or good enough to fulfil
your dreams, your expectations, to satisfy
your unbalanced needs.

Unbalanced: am I too steady for you,
lacking in energy or risk-taking skills,
too mundane? Some widen their nets
for lovers, new minds to patch up the flaws.

Conspiracies Fail

Your multitude of conspiracies betray you.
Take your self-inflicted silences: however
efficiently you prescribe them, their effects
are measurable. Their cost is measured in
saddening ways. You lose. You do not gain.
The ones you love lose too.

Your self-imposed rules and regulations, your
self-imposed justifications, "instant" justifications,
forever betray you. They betray you because
they simply do not work, effects are negative.
Your impotence at every challenge freezes you.
It angers you with such intensity. Your silences
create but myth and fantasy, like stereotypes
they're often false. You're not sure when or how.

These secrecies deny debate and strategy.
Secrecies deny a sharing, perceptions and
evaluations forever warped. Outcomes
are void, devoid of enrichment. The risk
is there: even those for whom you care
may be betrayed, by conspiracies that fail.

Sisters of Nazareth

The guilt they left her with had manifestations
in plenty: how to bring up her kids, how to enjoy
and support her husband. Her alcohol and drugs
had hardly helped.

And after her funeral her mum and family
(no mention of dad) wondered what they'd
done wrong. Of course, they hadn't. They'd long
ago abandoned their gods and crucifixes. Strange
how their guilt vanished too.

Sisters of Nazareth – pre-dalek, akin to stultified
rulers of far away times, with scrolls so outmoded.
Hidden from those more fulfilled: hidden from passion
and loving, a diabolical waste of beauty and potential.
What fraternity had they nurtured in those tragic lives.
Tragic for my cousin with her damaged and shortened life.

We've Spliced the Umbilicus

Clear deliberations are neither certainties
nor truths. Mere evidence you'd prefer
to ignore is a righteous challenge.

What is self-possession? Part of some
dimension: an identity? Esteem? Or arrogance?
Even a blindness to uncertainty.

Conflicts with partners that once tried to love
are trials we almost contrive to fail at.
We accept them as placental misgivings, life
between lives, ephemeral, a parasite
and host in one.

They launch those inheritances, they grovel
for identity, empowerment, space (or should
that be territory?) and their false dynasties.

Vessels feed these agitated minds, like
motorway traffic that grid-locks towns.

Perspectives and priorities redeem the self,
determine dilemmas. They unfacet each lens
that vivifies each focus, zoom away from
each image. They frost-out each fresco,
stifle each familial icon. We've spliced
the umbilicus that strangles our esteem.

Faceless Icons and Spurious Ideals

We haul ourselves towards those faceless icons,
infused with spurious ideals, a kind of mesmeric
kedging. The attraction may seem real, a motivating
force, with appeal, a force that projects you
towards this irresolute focus.

Icons are symbolic: representing features, distortions
or aberrations, an illusion or mirage... a philosophic
hoax! But icons are like that. They may appeal
to those who fail to question, the gullible, complacent.
They keep our artists and poets exploring their medium,
escaping scholastic and cultural constraints.

Ideals are notional: maybe conceptual, hypothetical,
something you feel will launch you to a goal. That may
be mythical, fantastical, totally false, but may also lead to
emancipation. Yet, for some, give kinds of guidance,
a direction to an end, however ill-defined
or inconclusive, worse still false.

Hamlet's Conundrum

Contingencies and conundrums are the stuff
of everyday life. Whatever the connotations
they'll determine routines and challenges.
Epiphanic episodes will create new
squabbles for sure.

Such quiddities may be at times quite fun;
scabrous deviations may test your vulnerability,
expose your hang-ups, stretch your
disjunctive logic.

Yet everyone survives, even when the cost
is high. But the problem is how you accept
your type of survival, your level of coping.
Has self-esteem become enriched, or mutilated?

That is what you have to know, and what you
have to internalize. Essentially, "to be or not to be".

Big Issues

Indifference is so indecisive, as if no care
in the world has been involved. Look at attitudes
to the destitute, the growing contingency
of the elderly in need of care; sick children
too. They do not deserve this wanton disarray
of planning where little of practical worth
evolves. Especially of the stealthily,
commercialized, vulgarized kind.

The slow poison of despair helps no-one,
breeds more indifference. Keeps those
who don't care in cleaner air.

With so little public respect for the down-and-outs,
and others disadvantaged, few are prepared
to sacrifice themselves. Persistent, positive
attitudes demand much energy, not just
conscience cash and dubious commitment.

If your clients are static with depression, despair
or low self-esteem they'll feel unfulfilled.
They require far more than smiling faces
or goodwill followed by desertion, or other
actions of no consequence.
These are big issues; not tawdry imaginings.

For Good or Ill

("Why should the family be the crucible of moral turpitude?" – Will Hutton)

No foetus has a moral status; there's no refinement yet
of "person". It is born the same, no moral comprehension,
no hint of judgement, no stratagems for right or wrong.

Later on may well become affectionate, co-operative, sociable
and warm. The family gets the credit! While others
destroy; they'll subjugate, insult and bully, will not accept
appraisal or support. They're from a turbulent family, truculent,
corrupt. The family gets the blame!

Those failing parents had parents too, or someone else's.
They're part of their community, however dysfunctional, however
uncooperative, deviant. No sense of fulfilment, achievement.

Parents are rarely alone in guiding their offspring. They
are part of a social amalgam, each component interacting,
somehow shaping children's lives, for good or ill.
That is society; society at large.

Personalized Peace

There is a peace, a peace where no-one suffers
remorse or guilt. Experiences devoid of acrimony
and bitterness. Vindictiveness does not arise; nothing
compulsive nor paranoid. Fears of delusional
pressures have gone; you feel so utterly free, released.

Your new alertness, from those neural pathways
with their special gateways, imagination extant, have no
filtering nor dilution. Your crystal openness and dazzle
enhance your intimate calm, your personalized peace.
You've composed yourself and evolved.

Are You Still Where You Were?

We all know how anguish sustains.
A pain is so real, remembered, reassembled
in your mind. Affects you. Traumatizes.
Though perceptions may change.

Your focus alters, you re-define the language
of interpretation. The world of "then" is different
from the world of "now". Recall may well
be disjointed, recoloured, shadows shortened,
sounds less harsh.

Scenery and seasons fluctuate, cascades continue
their fall, the air may become more turbulent...
Are you still where you were? If so then move on.

Holding Together

The Higgs-Boson glue that holds the universe
together, us too, is immensely small. Yet
its impact is truly colossal. Your personal self
and other inadvertent fillings, are the very
components that need a holding together.

We have our skills of communication, but
they may well veer into fantasies and dreams.
Also could be nervy ponderings, blips of
distorted images, whatever. Variety is there,
intensity, occasionally quiescence and transience.
The scale and range exceed imagination.

In early years we conquer gaucheness, anxiety,
false pride. We learn to make those early
observations, voyeurism, even stalking.
Our selfish entrapments slow us down, disturb.
An innocent gaze, a blank expression. We
evaluate, adjust, and ponder on ourselves,
the galaxies, the universe. We hold it all together.

Wartime Hens

Yes, I remember the hens. Dad bought them in '39.
Their eggs had golden yolks, sometimes two.
The shells were hard. Chalky soil.

I boiled potato peel, stirred in the meal – a low-grade
flour. They ate with fury, such heat and pain on icy
mornings: primary needs overcame hell.

One died. The hens attacked me when I tried to
remove it. The cock stood by, no care for a corpse
who'd been such a part of his harem.

I whitewashed their hut inside, creosoted the outside.
Straw in the nest-boxes was searched each day for eggs.
Only a kid I was then. Tuppence a day for my work.

The routine was simple, sometimes a chore, but, Oh!
Such a reward. We pickled the eggs in waterglass*
and stored them in a giant pot under the stairs.

Their droppings were quite a contrast, but the crops
near by were always so rich, robust, from this elemental
manure. But once a bird stopped their laying, crack!

We'd sacrifice it for food. Chew it to the bone.
The wishbone trembled in the hand: the guilt
of exploitation trepanned the mind.

(sodium or potassium silicate, a preservative)

The Waffling Iron

Mid 1940s: I remember the war. I also remember
the waffling iron. We buttered the bread: "you spread it
all on then you spread it all off," said Mum… Butter
then was rationed.

You pressed the buttered sides outwards into the waffle iron's
two moulds. Between the two slices of the skew-cut bread,
the dry sides, you placed some cheese. The handles were
brought together to close the moulds over your back-to-front
sandwich. This cut the crusts right off. We'd eat them later.

You held by two handles your waffling iron and placed it
in the fire. Well, above it. If the coals were too hot you burnt
your hands. The cheese would melt and leak out, catch on fire.
Best to withdraw it in time.

Open the halves of the iron device, and there was your waffle.
Your supper, your ration, your washing up.
And on waged the war; in Europe, as well as at home.

Gold-plated Nibs

Fountain pens were so smooth to operate.
No scratching like those awful steel nibs
you dipped into inkpots/ink wells so hard
not to overfill. They readily spilt on our desks.

Each fountain pen had a reservoir that held
its ink. Five or six mls would last a day
or two. Left-handers still smudged their work;
you needed blotters, special paper that absorbed
excesses. The warmth from your hand made
the ink in the reservoirs expand – then it would
puddle and spoil your own presentation.

The gold stopped the nibs from rusting. Did not
alter the quality or neatness of lines. Nor did it
alter clarity. Just elevated your dreams
of better taste, a touch of class.

Bequeathments

The graffiti on my brain is sourced by my lifestyle,
part imposed, part cultivated. Components
may be compatible, sometimes not so. The detail
may be overlooked, the constructions may entail
selection, assembly, trials.

The flexible aftermath may be quirky, short on
connectedness, even over-manicured. Yet somehow
functional. Individuals may yearn for kinds of transcendence.
While others more oblique will be translucent even
transparent, and will not yield to delusional practices.

The outcome may be full of nostalgia, resentment,
anger, but may well be affable, unselfish. Variety
defines our uniqueness, individuality,
priorities and preferences.

The mosaic in the end, like confetti, like graffiti,
comes to rest. Your pattern once fixed determines
longevity, outcome, bequeathments.

Your Private Tattoos

("so long the reach of death" – Rebecca West)

Don't steep yourself in the anguish of doubt
or disbelief; open your self to yourself
and be sure. The violence of pain and doubt
may be prolonged, an endless vertigo, like
the vertigo of dying, a long way down.

But moments in between are crucial:
when you recall your past it's like dissecting
a fossil. It uncurls its sequences, its history.
The more you recall the more you appreciate
its substance.

Don't waste time on illusory calm or vacant
promises and expectations. The stains of life,
your private tattoos, are but trees on a country
stroll, never the whole of reality.

They help with perceptions of beauty, deter
self-doubt if clinically sad. Solemnity has little
value, a great facade. But there to be ignored.
Turn your back on it. Avoid all its shadows. Move on.

A Subconscious Sorting

("Courage is not enough. Distractions are also necessary" – Voltaire)

Do we really comprehend the nature of courage,
its special features? Do we classify and link it
with probity and daring? Fortitude or gallantry?
I would like to see tenacity, intrepidity, ardour.

Because we can't define it clearly we'll never be sure
if it's there, operating. Panache and chivalry won't count,
nor dedication. If that's not enough dare we ask
"enough of what?"

Which distractions would we expect or desire to help us
focus, show commitment? Would maladjustment
or aberrations help? Obsessions or infatuation? Surely
lateral thinking would score, extending the genius
of those bipolar. Some of those dyslexic too.

The manic phase would highlight the extremes
and eccentricities; the depressive phase would guarantee
regeneration and consolidation, a subconscious sorting.
The bipolar affliction must surely maintain.

Incidental Fillings

A silent stare, a vacant smile, an inadvertent
gesture, contact of an eye or two... Can we
actually observe such things without participation?
By being there an interaction must occur,
subconsciously perhaps.

Even being lost in a crowd will make you part
of it. Its size will have a range of influences.
A crowd at a concert or match, so single-minded,
but differing responses. Postures change; some
will be relaxed, while others fidget.

Being part of someone else's social scheme,
an incidental cog in a complex machine, gives
you a focus all your own. Friend or stranger,
searching questions may arise. Replies may well
not gel. May not take place. You may be
totally ignored. You feel the pressures there.

These incidental fillings of time and space are
the components of your being, awareness, mind.

Slowness

My slowing down mode takes so much longer
now. I await new energy that fails to arrive.
Thinking time. Thinking time. Sad time.
Lost time. Less time.

You actually need more time to slow, to slow
right down. Each shred of recall takes longer
to download and process, to give it the special
cloak it deserves.

Each strip of memory has to be unfurled, reprocessed,
re-identified and separated from the fantasies
and social factions of influence. Especially those
moral bigotries you were once embroiled in
that affected your interplay, analysis and rejections.

Adolescence was a time for rejections both real
and imagined, both really hard to handle. Those
young folk hadn't had that age of parents before,
nor the experience of coping with their inexplicable
fantasies and dilemmas. But time was not a problem then.

Not like now, the slowness itself is slowing, one's perception
of slowness is becoming more blurred. The memories
of yesterday's slowness gets harder to recall.

Moments of Wisdom

Will the fading light of life affect us
in those dimming years? Some of us
become more rigid as we age,
while others simply prevaricate.

Ponderously we seem to recognize
that the faultless lustre of earlier years
has lost its shine; at times there seems
an emotional void.

Others sense a creeping disparity, a kind
of tingling emptiness that envelopes them
like an evening cloud. Is their taciturnity
but a make-shift apology for slowing down?

A reticence pervades: one is counting the days
to that final epicedium! Yet, despite these tedious
trajectories we have our moments: occasionally
jocular, moments of wisdom, irony.

Hidden Agendas

You will not desire an indecisive end;
the death itself is out of your control.
But pondering on the "if" and "when",
the "how" and its duration you'll probably
want to leave that out.

Any kind of limbo, hidden agendas,
ambiguities and lies, will create anxiety.
Opinions will clash with facts, morbidity
with false hopes.

Self-pity and sorrow are a waste of time.
All they do is magnify uncertainty and gloom.

A comfort zone can only be conjecture,
though pain can be controlled. A fear
of inactivity, inability to get things done,
a drifting in and out of sane awareness,
all can get you down.

Like any agendas, hide them and your confidence
will plummet. The limbo you're left in will defy
any comfort zone. Indecisiveness will
eventually leave you cold.

Cremations Are so Unselective

I look at my ageing hands.
The angle of light creates a moonscape:
ridges that branch and pulsate across the dried-up
flood plains. The hairs are like burnt out
tree trunks from the Somme.

Occasional scars from gardening remind
me of the fragility of flesh, its colourful
healing, its lumpy disregard for aesthetic
judgements.

Each hair is slightly bent,
though not with the symmetry of cornfields,
not with the smoothness of a feline pelt
say of a Burmese or Persian beauty.

The length of hairs is variable, brown, grey
or black. The skin itself is like a finely
wrinkled sheet of tin-foil, stained by
the sizzling stews: oven-black putrefactions.

Cremations are so unselective.

Flirting with Shapely Old Birds

It's the slowing down that gets me. The slow,
almost imperceptible changes, in one direction too.
Your movements, your planning, your daily
thinking, frustrations all seem to take longer.

Do you remember Sylvester? Victor Sylvester.
He tempered the nimble footwork of dancers:

SLOW, SLOW ,QUICK, QUICK, SLOW...
and made his mark world over.

I have left the quick bits for ever! Even slowness
is slowing. The soles, the heels, no longer swivel,
the body and limbs have no rhythm, precision,
nor uniform tack.

When the band strikes up I no longer feel the beat.
There are some my age who'll take to the floor
and float around smiling. They seem totally free
of those toe-crushing misalignments that ended
my flirting with shapely old birds from
the other side of town.

Welcome New Beacons

As spouses we parted, dying the death
that seemed somehow determined.
Life's mournings had culminated, quite
patchily. Not much real ash. We dusted
ourselves down and marched on.

We'd retain our volcanic range of mountains,
strive to push up new peaks; we'd scale them
alone and confident. Both of us,
no longer a pair.

A pair of individual isolates, divergent, diverging,
diverged; disparate and ready. Ready to aspire
to and welcome new beacons, not cremations
of lost souls. But floodlights with direction,
lenses polished, more refined.

We'd erupt, mould our new lava. The fertile
ranges will germinate new horizons, bury the dead,
create new lives. Welcome new beacons.

Those Final Notes

Winds whistle through their scores, electrify.
Electrify as frets of prismic rainbows
and create their beautiful distortions
of harmony. They startle our ears.

Echoes ever lost, voices dumb as ever,
then silences of eternity beyond the shivers
of winter, shuffling into spring. May be
your final spring, your silent spring. Yet
nature's music as ever remains.

While we, extant, will languish and linger,
amidst the limping clouds, our maundering
rapport dying slowly, grasping those final notes.

Just Love

Wrinkles are said to be the signatures of death:
is that insight or idle speculation? Does it matter?
We've all heard the stertorous breathing of heavy
smokers, facing their countdown.

Once your days are numbered it's too late to restore
self-pity. Emphysema, thrombosis, ischemia,
cancer... take your pick.

Your time will soon be up, whatever. You've lived
your life, its hopes and aspirations, its tragedies
and vulnerabilities. You rely on friendships
and artefacts, cultivate a kind of equanimity,
do your best to remain calm and serene.

But be passionate to the full when you meet
those vital challenges; especially those challenges
with your special friends. No parodies,
no profanities. Just love.

No need for fears of eternity and other forms
of falsehood and innuendo.

Life and Death Are like That

Memories are lost like broken antiques,
never to be reconstructed: priceless gems
in their own eternity without recall.

Survivors may sift their truths and lies
and re-distribute them like reshuffled cards.
The images remaining are embossed, over-polished
like reglued fragments of damaged porcelain.

Vibrations of humour, with touches of ridicule,
mark the echoes from a labyrinth. Strained,
with truth that is furtively diluted.

Life and death are like that. Memories of life
are shrunken; memories of death seem focussed
yet minimal. Heartaches that pulse through
your ribs will deafen and deaden
as they scour the mind.

Something like the white cells of your blood
that engulf your demons. Oblations, if you like,
to an absent friend.

Your Transience Percolates

Each building echoes its past – the timbers creak,
the masonry cracks, distorts and spalls. This all
disturbs complacency – that's far too comfortable.
Not so much like ghosts but memories and speculation.
People there had lives, experiences, opinions
and arguments.

Their certainties, prejudices, aspirations
all arrived, with time and effort, then ceased to be.
So soon to be forgotten. Sometimes, too, to be denied.
Your transience percolates through-out your life;
it ceases with you when you die.

Silent Years

The immaculate hearse glides by,
its manicured freight drowned in petals,
a tribute to the one who no longer breathes.

Silent years look on, wilting flowers
soon sigh their last. Observers reconstrue
their guilt and lifelessly follow the protocol
of mourning: this pondering on death
and the dead.

Correct yourself; re-align; question
the motives that drive you on. Will you
know when you've arrived? Direction
and duration? Are they clear to you?

Grieving is slow, so slow. It can't
be rehearsed. But you'll live on for awhile,
while petals fall.

Before He'd Arrived

Heart-massage failed.
The haemorrhage was too severe
An ECG was almost flat.
The rhythm of breathing
had signalled that final fall
from the crazy heights
of failed reasoning.

When Mum said "I've forgotten
what I've remembered" and saw
old friends, long-deceased,
at her bedside, they'd not been
resurrected. Just rejects
from her damaged mind.

The doors that slammed and banged
were the Germans again, bombing
her town. The yearning for Dad
was to invite him for tea.
She died on his birthday
before he'd arrived.

Survivors

(On the news that there have now been more suicides amongst the British survivors of the Falklands war than deaths direct from the war itself, 07:2002)

Hollyhocks stare at you
like eyes in photographs.
They notice your eager gaze.

You've seen them before:
Anne Hatherway's cottage,
Victorian postcards,
clutching the walls
of thatched homes.

Always this hankering
after the past: for happier
yesterdays. Even the Empire.

Tell that to relatives and friends
of the Falkland survivors
who killed themselves
in order to end their utter despair.

Plankton

The lurching and rocking of waves will swallow
you, swallow you as it torments the sands and shells.
While seaweeds sway and toss their history, the jetsam
of tarnished trades, the flotsam of civilisation's anguish
and dross, you'll swallow the sea and ponder your demise.

Engulfed like wonders of old encased in fearful forests,
dark with wolves and boars, denying your points
of navigation. You'll choke on life's plankton.

When Pain Is so Deceptive

Those absent calls just nurture the emptiness.
Absence, like social silence, does not allow the filtering
away of my apprehensions. I try not to reflect
on injustices and suffering, despite my loss of composure.

This personal distress only magnifies my indecision.
Your silence may be legitimate, but if I have no indication
how can perspective be calming? We know the old adage
that sweetness can emerge from grief, but how can that
concord and joy be recognised when pain is so deceptive.

Profundity needs no sophistication. Your patient waiting
may well demand yet more patience! You may even decide
to call it a day. But if your judgements are full of error
you'll then have to cope with guilt. And you'd question your guilt.

Uniforms and Power

Degenerates, dolts, misfits... put them in a uniform
and their behaviour will change! Their image will change.
Their attitudes change. They expect to have more authority
and POWER.

They won't just shuffle around, they'll march or stomp.
They'll expect to be admired, deferred to, stepped aside
for. Will people around believe what these "officers"
now say? Does their enhanced self-perception and greater
confidence protect them? Need they listen so much,
or reason at all?

Would these uniformed urbanites apologise for their errors?
Will they become the archetypal bullies? Maybe now they'll
manufacture populist one-liners, or use their simplistic
solutions incautiously.

Will their facile decisions, blithe spirits, indifference to
evidence... make their voices change? They might become
more shrill, harsher, coarser, deeper, louder. Will formulaic
judgements be their forte? And how about a degenerate
innocence? Perhaps they'll edit out those cryptic lies
with less caution.

Some traffic wardens and prison officers may need questioning.
Not so much our nurses. School uniforms? The jury is still out
on that one. Why be UNIFORM? Don't we want our offspring
to become individuals rather than conformists? Aldous Huxley's
epsilons were standardised! It's all a matter of image and self-
respect – some say. Yet they don't, after all, have to always be right.

A Giant Gateau

History's intrepid chaos has somehow created civilisations.
A world of fragmentation it seems with a perpetual jolting
of principles and values. Were these not once thought
to be irrefutable?

A great divide has evolved: tools for wielding power,
and attitudes that may demand a liberal leaning. A right
and left in politics: dichotomies are rife.

Polished language shapes the lies and ambiguities, puts
poultices on reason, helps you choose your preferences
and prejudices. A bit like the Vatican's Office of Dogma!
Assertive bigotries are hidden deep in sinister inventiveness.

Something like a giant gateau hiding poison. Helping you
they say, but devious and distorted, making talent itself
seem so dubious, deceptive. Fascists killed the staff at
universities. Communists were the same, they killed their
artists, poets, journalists too... anyone with independent minds.

Intellectuals were seen to live on wine and cake!
If they weren't perceived to understand your bigotry
they'd not become your friends.

Pristine Paradise

Impalpable ironies, parodies and satire, suspended
disavowal and disbelief, with a muteness of sensitivity:
That's what some people accept without question.
Giant books that no longer rule or impose limitations:
they held too much authority with their ancient sagas.

Yet millions are squeezed into these blind bunkers,
these irrelevant, outmoded documents that incarcerate minds.
There's a mixing of the immiscible. We are after all receivers
of these gospels and cant. They're supposed to present us with
wisdom, authenticity. Yet what happens is people get soaked
and warped with prejudiced opinions, the alternatives to reason.

Tautness of the nerves, string-tight tension that holds you in,
keeps you unrelaxed. Honest doubts! They'll give you false
security. Why lose sleep with rattling uncertainties
that punctuate and puncture placidity in the realms
of delicate and pristine paradise?

Barbed Bons Mots

Predictably barbed are those bons mots,
especially about predictability, and how
to avoid it. Something deadly dissenting
is a choice: like conceptual art!

Is it art? The artists said it is.
Would you ask a plumber to judge
a surgeon's skills?

Are certain concepts too big or too complex
for public eyes? Perhaps descriptive language
gets reshaped to fool us. So much humbug
and absurdity to make a nonsense sound
feasible (take politicians and theocrats!).
Entraps those gullible and many more.

Ideas are frangible, meanings are fractal
and devious. Why be predictable?

Secular Reality

Let us purge ourselves of the brawling
hierarchies of ecclesiastic celebrants
and acolytes. So much of their cadaverous
sweetness rests on falsehood
and demeaning ritual.

Their followers get intoxicated by the propaganda;
lose track of sagacity; condemn themselves
to a world of unreason; sink into subjective
idealism. Such is the banality and barrenness
of blind belief.

If only they'd review their tenets and credence,
question their resistance to secular reality,
attempt to evolve.

A New Armageddon

Few people will die under 90 in a few years
from now. Herds of self-pitying nerds will plague
the world with their ailments and crazy demands.

The pavements will clog with electric wheelchairs.
Crashes will mutilate the elderly and overweight
kids. Hysterical mums will rant and rave.

When something wrecks the waves in the air
and mobiles won't work, computers will lie
to us, aircraft will no longer navigate...

Where will taxes come from to pay for this demise
of agility, the slower aged, the helpless
centenarians, the chronic boredom?

Schools will close for lack of children.
Jobs will not equate with available skills.
A new Armageddon will dawn.

Mum's Infamous One-liners

Stop that hacking cough, she'd say to Dad.
You obstinate old bugger, you're dead
but won't lie down. Get out and do something.
You sit around all day like a fart in a colander.

You can get rid of that dog too. It jumps up at you.
Don't want any monsters around here.

And stop looking in that bucket in the bathroom,
she'd said to me. That's women's things and not
for your eyes. So don't keep asking questions
then you'll get no lies. Whoever told you that?
Even your Dad doesn't know.

Just look at those horses out there. Those girls
should be riding side-saddle. Not decent with their
legs as wide apart as that.

Mrs T. Came round last night about her Audrey.
Said you'd looked inside her knickers.
Girls are different. They don't have a willy. So
leave it at that. But don't show others your own.

Hallucinations

Minds can play tricks. Like a scene from a film
where the actors step out from the screen
and join the audience. An interactive dream,
sometimes with the wrong characters.

I'd had my operation; the anaesthetic hadn't quite
worn off. The woman there I thought was my wife.
I fondled her, much to her surprise. For just a moment
my dream moved on.

I was wrong. My wife was there but I'd not taken that in.
Peace reigned eventually, apologies all round.

No psychosis; no deception; no opportunism.
A dream-world, melancholic, a mental wandering.
Somewhat fatuous, absurd even. Yet an air of intangibility
prevailed, a mirage, sophistry, irrelevant once
it had all passed by.

Such emptiness. Even a conundrum of subjectivity.

High Fliers

Nice sitting over the wing.
You can watch for rivets
popping as you hurtle through
clouds and step up the strata
of altitude.

I wonder too if the pilot
knows how to land this one
on one engine, or skim across
mud-flats with no wheels, do
a belly-flop without turning
turtle so that inflatables can be
shot out on time.

Remember too to stub out
your fags, kick
off high-heels
and jump out feet first – sod
the oxygen.

A bit like getting a new job,
not knowing the parameters.
Flying high's the easy bit.
It's when you plummet to despair
and realise on this last occasion
you'll never be short-listed again.

A New Perspective

Those dripping sores of self-immolation
no longer shock. We've conquered their matrix
of blind alleys. There's more demand for risk
and challenge now. Any din will simply echo
as in a labyrinth.

The world must be encountered: emancipation
must replace the unreal exploitation that's
crippled those deemed inferior. While those
deluded and naïve need a new perspective.

Dying Images

(Alicante, Spain)

Not a shimmer in the palm fronds,
just the shushing of waves on
the shoreline gravel. The lighthouse
blinks its scanning eye, keeps watch;
penetrates the early sea fret.

Gentle dove-song competes with
the raucous gulls. Bells bang out their
signals, call conformers in to shed
their secret guilts. While priests hide
theirs, fixate the minds of their uncritical
flocks. Dying images and rituals strafe
the fantasies of shrinking congregations.

Those Glorious Adventures

Cloistering them into cohorts of conformists, bland
yes-men (& women!), strafing their innocence
and curiosity is the outcome of rigid teaching.
You can hear the cries in the wafts of chalk dust;
they become so muted. Where are aspirations, metaphors
and meanings? How can the young express themselves?

By accident or default teachers are often just stealthy
predators of the kids they are said to care for. Those
children are tricked by coercion and humiliation,
didactic approaches shaping their victims' replies
to questions by subtle manipulation.

Casual dishonesty permeates the classroom ethos, false
dichotomies, wilful obtuseness. Where are those glorious
adventures that enable escape from those deferential
murmurings and moral masquerades?

No longer is there need for tyranny. Perhaps there
wasn't before. Socrates avoided self-abasement, sourness,
sardonic double-standards. Some students resist: their
tenacious obstinacy and contemptuous reactions will not
enhance co-operation and harmony.

Yet, incongruity can be creative, sadness overwhelmed.
Essential to allow each child to aspire, to become.
Differences and independence must be heralded for fresher
appraisals. A student must be open to the world of thought,
ideas and principles, and the dissidence that emerges from
openness in debate and systematic questioning.

Dissent

There are social incompatibilities, tribal values,
racial dichotomies, religious feuds, patriotism,
nationalistic priorities... all with sub-groups
and factions.

Then there are political wrangles, economic mal-
functions, territorial decisions, expansionism,
multi-national interceptions. And do not forget
those global conglomerates controlling quality,
sales, and the unfair distribution of goods.

We also have stratifications and dissent.
Dissent! That mega-phenomenon. It somehow
motivates democratic procedures. Pretentiousness
and dishonesty get monitored, seeking out the verbal
bubble-wrap of schemes of controls. There are
always conventions of controls. Restrictions in
practice. They mesmerise and satisfy so few.
Though alternatives seem worse.

How could regenerated trust be guaranteed?
International sales of weapons? Sophisticated
technology, the network of manipulated deception
and more false "certainties". Yet we still seek
security where no single weapon need apply.
An ultimate thought, still unresolved.

Obsequious Conformity

I'm paralysed by procrastinating pulpiteers.
The pace of their slow and mediocre
perambulations appalls me.

When decisions have to be made and actions
to initiate they'll rely on the indefensible
platitudes and mythical moralizing that cut
no ice; well not with those with reason who think!

They'll counterfeit their language to entrap
their flocks. Their reverence and deference
to some remote agency just will not do.
The maundering and louring clouds
that stifle thought must blow away.

We've grown beyond obsequious conformity.
We want our voices heard.

A Smile of Exultation

The abuses of doctrine and dogma will stifle you.
Those maundering clouds of gloom must never
be allowed to linger. They'll creep in through
your shutters and muffle your mind. They'll waft
down your chimneys and pollute your air.

A cloying life of ill-perceived sin and fear will cripple
your mind-sets with guilt. Your self-empowerment will be
sequestered: why bow beneath this dishonest burden?

Seek the romance of Odysseus, bury the tragic memories
from the Iliad, seek hard evidence, aspire to a review of reality
and deny the anachronisms of spurious belief. Let your vacant
smile become a joyous, self-confident smile of exultation.

A New Synthesis

Let the world touch you. Don't withdraw
like a snail to its shell. Don't cringe and sag
into numb retreat or dumb introspection.

Unresolved agonies may fester; their dripping
sores of self-immolation can become
the gangrenous rot of self-pity. Fight it.
Resist it. It is crushable.

Ravines of fear and uncertainty are often
not there at all, just subliminal mysteries, sub-
conscious doubts, awaiting your mindedness
to emerge from the wallowings of self-deception
and pessimism.

Let every matrix of blind alleys
become a new synthesis.

A Buckled Mosaic

Those unaware may well be benevolent
but hopelessly preoccupied. Preoccupied
with narrow perceptions of honour, duty,
deference. The empty words and blurred
pictures in their squalid journals have lost
their price-tags: all are distorted.

Those so immersed in conceit have
such cruel perceptions. They're totally
unaware of the imposed dilution of their
independence. A buckled mosaic of
treacherous creeds and prophecies has been
dangled in front of them so long now
they've lost the will to question, to challenge.

Secular Transilience

Don't ever swear allegiance! That only generates
authority totally devoid of authenticity. Like
all tradition it's fine in books. Just as antiquity
is fine in museums. We've outgrown the flatness
of moral turpitude and all those bickering cults.

The perpetrators of the antiquated texts, with all their
supercilious disdain, no longer keep to their own
flawed rules. They've lost their credibility. The quiet
guilt of public presumptions needs no statue or plaque.
Nor hints of false respectability.

Even the profligate buildings have wilted beneath
the concrete and glass of a secular transilience.

You Slice-up False Logic

Cognitive dissonance is a mercurial sword:
it cuts through conformity and degenerate
mythology. Like a raptor, with its pinnacle
of aerial predation, mental agitations
are constructive realignments.

When a hawk feeds it destroys. When you
change your mind you eliminate distortions,
incongruities, fictions and fallacies. Not
unlike dissidence where you challenge
nonsensical norms.

You disturb complacency, agitate anomalies,
crucify conundrums. You attack all convention,
you slice-up false logic.

Conformity Corrupts

Icons keep things moving: dependent
as they are on superstition, a pluralistic
ignorance and dubious ritual.

This global cult insists on, commands,
demands rigidity, unquestioning
blind loyalty...

Where are introspection, effective
communication, knowledge? Semantic
trickery can be so impure when
dispersed among the gullible.

But ritual reinforces: diehard dictats
do dictate. And flocks conform. Dissidents
are quietly dispersed, dispensed with,
destroyed. Conformity corrupts.
Omerta rules!

Indolence

Dithering, pitching and rolling, twitching
and wavering keep your audience alert and waiting.
But floundering may cost lives, may cripple resolutions
that change history. Dilemmas are unresolved.

The pace of procrastination paralyses me! How
can the making of decisions be so slow? If evidence
is so meagre your resolutions will be temporal.
Conclusions after all can always be changed.

These are the outcomes of indolence.

Silence and Darkness

Silence and darkness will sometimes wear masks.
Nothing there is preternatural, no special insight,
no exclusiveness. These are but fantasies of dreamers.

But masks created by reflections, unidentified stimuli,
variable perceptions, are still there. They may disturb you.

They may even evoke an invisible pain, a tension,
a disconcerting uncertainty that agitate and maybe
frighten. Yet rarely grotesque. But always be prepared
for the unexpected, the uninvited; and do not assume
that magic is involved. At least they wouldn't hurt you
for long. Defy those masks.

We all know of silence and darkness: they each may be
ponderous even ferocious. They do not always have
an interface like oil on water. It may be more like anger
on a smiling face, something somehow dishonest,
lugubrious, mutilated by vulgar verbosity. Even a mere
tendril, antenna, polyp are but specimens of life after all,
like earthbound stars. Defy those masks.

In Order to Control

("the only indecency was in the mind" – Jacob Epstein)

Take prudery: the moral loading we insert into phrases and expressions
to make others feel guilty, under par, simply to control them. We treat
them as socially inferior. Actually it's worse than that.
They are labelled as inhibited, withdrawn.

Then there's respectability. Imagine a woodlouse cautioning its young
on conduct with other woodlice. For us it's little more than snobbery,
elitism, the pomposity some prefer. Creates barriers, and many folk
like to exclude those outside these benchmarks and barriers.
Yet claim superiority over woodlice!

And honour: that dubious system of merit. So much used for dividing
and ruling, creating the partitions that fragment our lives,
however arbitrary. Try asking if the prurient are really inferior to prudes!

You'd never expect democracy in the uniformed services: hierarchical
ranks insist on forcing others of lower ranks to defer. So when
the major says "fire" you'd not hold things up
for a referendum. Did we really need that war in the first place?
How were decisions made?

So why do we rank and grade ourselves? Why do those in higher tiers
have greater privilege? Equality was once thought to ease those
divisions that created resentment, envy and aggression.

We invent the worst in ourselves. No other creature insults his kind
or plans the demise of others. And some make scatty rules and
regulations, stultify imagination.

We practise this divisive need to classify, the greatest indecency
of them all, in order to control.

Make-up on a Cancerous Skin

There's a gullibility gene that makes you
adore things supernatural. It helps you
to incarcerate minds, including your own.

The problem arising is one of floating
mirages, that inveigh against what you
perceive as convulsions of logic and reason.

There are rivulets, rills and runnels, refluxes,
rapids and roller-coasters that dilute
all mainstream intellect. You end up with
flaccid obedience to formulaic judgements,
totally devoid of compassion: like paint
on rotting wood or make-up
on a cancerous skin.